This Doodle By Number Belongs To

....

By Doodle Lovely

To practice any art,
no matter how well or
badly, is a way to
make your soul grow.
So do it.

KURT VONNEGUT

www.DoodleLovely.com

HELLO!

I am so delighted you are here!

You don't have to be an artist to enjoy the positive
benefits of being creative - just start Doodling and the act of
doing will help you become more mindful and stay in the now.

This book was created with you in mind. Providing
small moments of playfulness as a gift you can give to yourself.
A pocket of time to spend and enjoy the simple pleasures
of relaxing will rejuvenate your mind.

Enjoy a new way to be soulful, connected and calm,
Doodling toward a healthier and happier you.

Doodle on!

Melissa x

WHY DOODLE?

It's true! People have been doodling for millennia. "Spontaneous drawing" has been studied and verified as a means to decrease stress in our lives.

Taking pen in hand and using the rhythmic motions of doodling, activates the relaxation response within the brain. Just the thing to calm the chaos!

Playfulness
Doodling promotes well-being, allowing you to lighten your mood whenever you feel overwhelmed.

Creative Freedom
Doodling is a workout for the mind that can help you focus on new ideas and bring fresh insights.

Improved Focus
Doodling is a simple and effective way to help you concentrate and process information.

DISCOVER THE BENEFITS OF DOODLING TODAY

Manage Emotions
Doodling is a safe method to evaluate unsettling emotions, converting jumbled feelings into a peaceful state of mind.

Greater Productivity
Doodling can refresh your mind and reset your thoughts, allowing for a greater sense of clarity.

Increased Memory
Studies indicate that while listening to others, the brain can recall 29% more information while doodling.

How to use your

DOODLE NUMBER

Pick up a pen, your favorite marker, or pencil of any color.

At the bottom of each example page there is a selection of five doodle patterns to choose from. Each pattern is circled and numbered.

Follow the numbers to create a doodle pattern on the opposite page. If you want to use more or less doodles, go for it!

Complete the *Doodle By Number*™ and touch it up to your satisfaction.

⑤

Feel free to make the doodle your own with your favorite shapes, lines and patterns. Even add color if you like. Doodle-riffic!

Follow the numbers to match your Doodles on the opposite page.

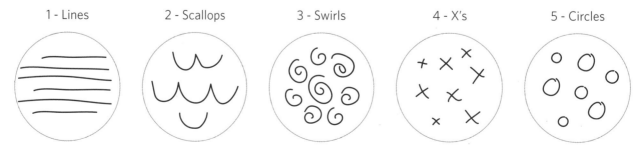

1 - Lines 2 - Scallops 3 - Swirls 4 - X's 5 - Circles

LIFE IS REALLY SIMPLE, BUT WE INSIST ON MAKING IT COMPLICATED.

CONFUCIUS

Follow the numbers to match your Doodles on the opposite page.

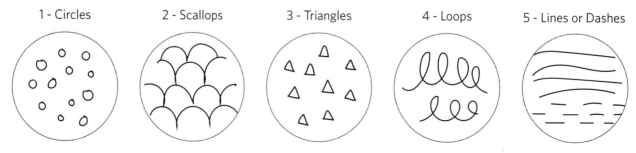

1 - Circles 2 - Scallops 3 - Triangles 4 - Loops 5 - Lines or Dashes

Change your thoughts
and you change your world.

NORMAN VINCENT PEALE

Follow the numbers to match your Doodles on the opposite page.

1 - Circles   2 - X's   3 - Loops   4 - Strokes   5 - Lines
(long, short or wavy)

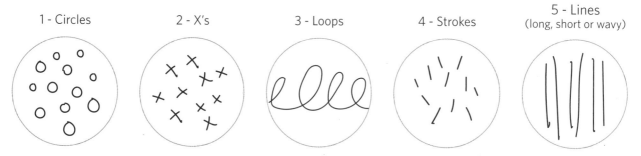

YOU CAN'T USE UP CREATIVITY.
THE MORE YOU USE, THE MORE YOU HAVE.

MAYA ANGELOU

Follow the numbers to match your Doodles on the opposite page.

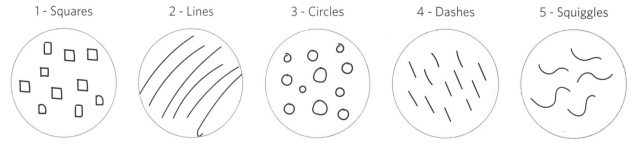

1 - Squares	2 - Lines	3 - Circles	4 - Dashes	5 - Squiggles

Happiness is a
state of activity.

ARISTOTLE

Follow the numbers to match your Doodles on the opposite page.

1 - Lines	2 - Loops	3 - Scallops	4 - X's	5 - Dashes

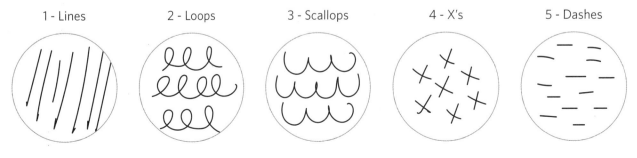

THERE IS NOTHING LIKE STAYING
HOME FOR REAL COMFORT.

JANE AUSTEN

Follow the numbers to match your Doodles on the opposite page.

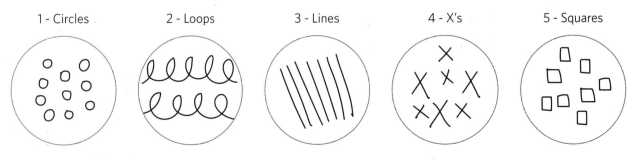

1 - Circles   2 - Loops   3 - Lines   4 - X's   5 - Squares

I am always doing that which I
cannot do, in order that I may
learn how to do it.

PABLO PICASSO

Follow the numbers to match your Doodles on the opposite page.

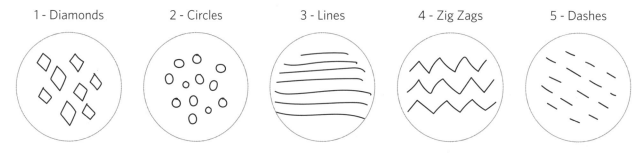

1 - Diamonds   2 - Circles   3 - Lines   4 - Zig Zags   5 - Dashes

LIFE ISN'T ABOUT FINDING YOURSELF. LIFE IS ABOUT CREATING YOURSELF.

NORMAN VINCENT PEALE

Follow the numbers to match your Doodles on the opposite page.

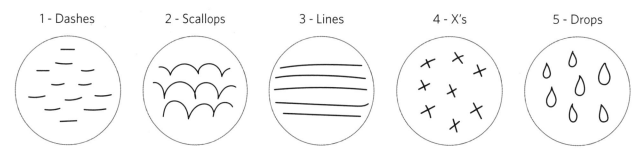

1 - Dashes 2 - Scallops 3 - Lines 4 - X's 5 - Drops

Fall in love with taking
care of yourself.

UNKNOWN

Follow the numbers to match your Doodles on the opposite page.

1 - Dashed Lines   2 - Spirals   3 - Dots   4 - Wavy Lines   5 - Double Scallops

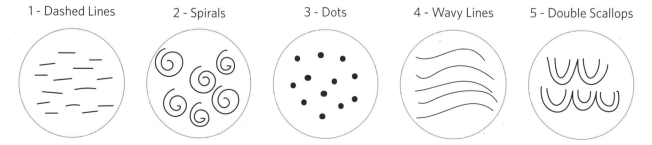

I'M NOT AFRAID OF STORMS FOR I'M LEARNING HOW TO SAIL MY SHIP.

LOUISA MAY ALCOTT

Follow the numbers to match your Doodles on the opposite page.

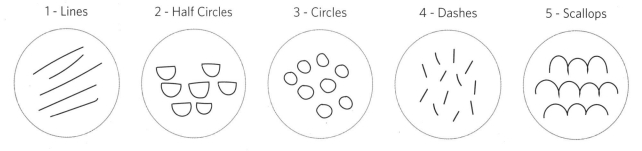

1 - Lines   2 - Half Circles   3 - Circles   4 - Dashes   5 - Scallops

Don't go through life,
grow through life.

ERIC BUTTERWORTH

Follow the numbers to match your Doodles on the opposite page.

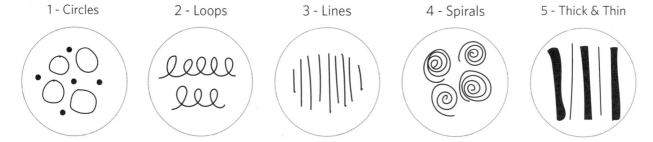

1 - Circles   2 - Loops   3 - Lines   4 - Spirals   5 - Thick & Thin

DON'T LET
YESTERDAY
TAKE TOO MUCH
OF TODAY.

WILL ROGERS

Follow the numbers to match your Doodles on the opposite page.

1 - Zig Zags   2 - Lines   3 - Peaks   4 - Circles   5 - Dashes

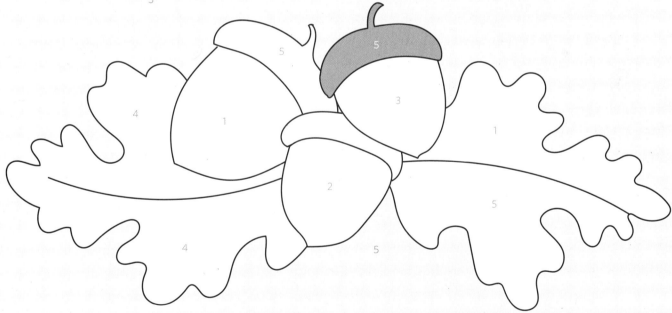

The best time for new beginnings is now.

UNKNOWN

Follow the numbers to match your Doodles on the opposite page.

1 - Solid Dots   2 - Circles   3 - Dashes   4 - Wavy Lines   5 - Scallops

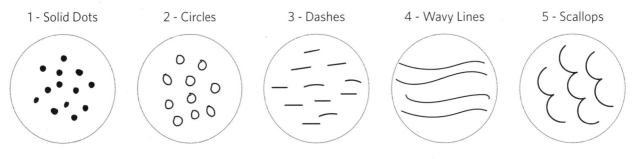

IN A WORLD FULL OF DOING,
IT IS IMPORTANT TO STOP AND JUST BE.

MELISSA LLOYD

Follow the numbers to match your Doodles on the opposite page.

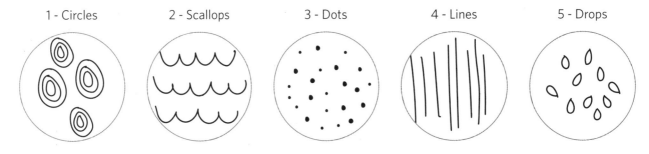

1 - Circles 2 - Scallops 3 - Dots 4 - Lines 5 - Drops

IT TAKES COURAGE TO GROW UP AND
BECOME WHO YOU REALLY ARE.

E. E. CUMMINGS

Follow the numbers to match your Doodles on the opposite page.

1 - Dots   2 -Drops   3 -Lines   4 - Scallops   5 - Triangles

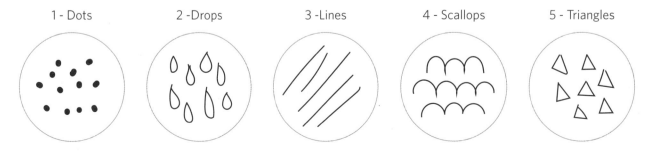

DON'T JUDGE EACH DAY BY THE HARVEST YOU REAP, BUT BY THE SEEDS THAT YOU PLANT.

ROBERT LOUIS STEVENSON

Follow the numbers to match your Doodles on the opposite page.

1 - Half Circles   2 - Lines   3 - Circles   4 - Dashes   5 - Drops

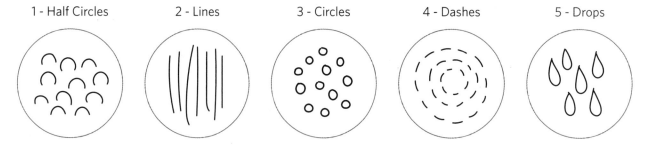

Every day is
a new beginning.
Take a deep
breath, smile and
start again.

UNKNOWN

Follow the numbers to match your Doodles on the opposite page.

1 - Circles 2 - Dashes 3 - Rectangles 4 - Lines 5 - Peaks

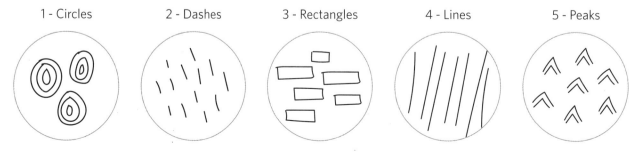

THE ONLY TIME YOU RUN OUT OF CHANCES
IS WHEN YOU STOP TRYING.

ALEXANDER POPE

Follow the numbers to match your Doodles on the opposite page.

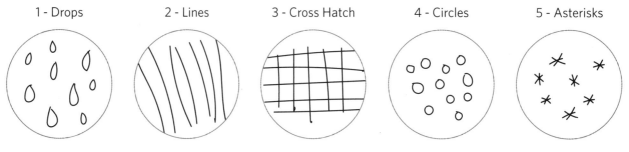

1 - Drops   2 - Lines   3 - Cross Hatch   4 - Circles   5 - Asterisks

Whatever you are,
be a good one.

ABRAHAM LINCOLN

Follow the numbers to match your Doodles on the opposite page.

1 - Lines   2 - Scallops   3 - Dashes   4 - Circles   5 - Squiggles

WHY FIT IN WHEN YOU
WERE BORN TO STAND OUT.

DR. SEUSS

Follow the numbers to match your Doodles on the opposite page.

1 - X's   2 - Lines   3 - Triangles   4 - Dashes   5 - Circles

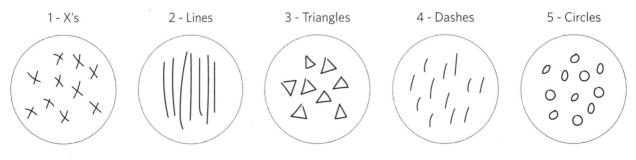

If life were predictable it would cease
to be life, and be without flavor.

ELEANOR ROOSEVELT

Follow the numbers to match your Doodles on the opposite page.

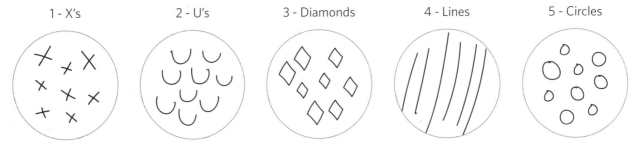

1 - X's   2 - U's   3 - Diamonds   4 - Lines   5 - Circles

YOU KNOW ALL THOSE THINGS YOU'VE
WANTED TO DO? YOU SHOULD GO DO THEM.

E.J. LAMPREY

Follow the numbers to match your Doodles on the opposite page.

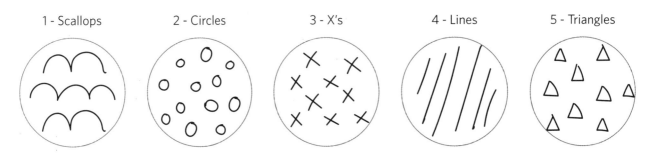

1 - Scallops   2 - Circles   3 - X's   4 - Lines   5 - Triangles

The best view
comes after the
hardest climb.

UNKNOWN

Follow the numbers to match your Doodles on the opposite page.

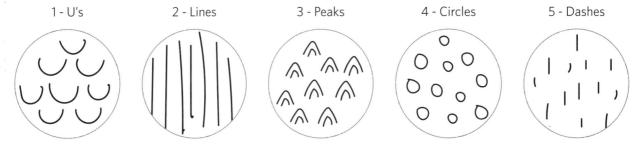

1 - U's   2 - Lines   3 - Peaks   4 - Circles   5 - Dashes

STOP OVER THINKING AND JUST DO THINGS.

UNKNOWN

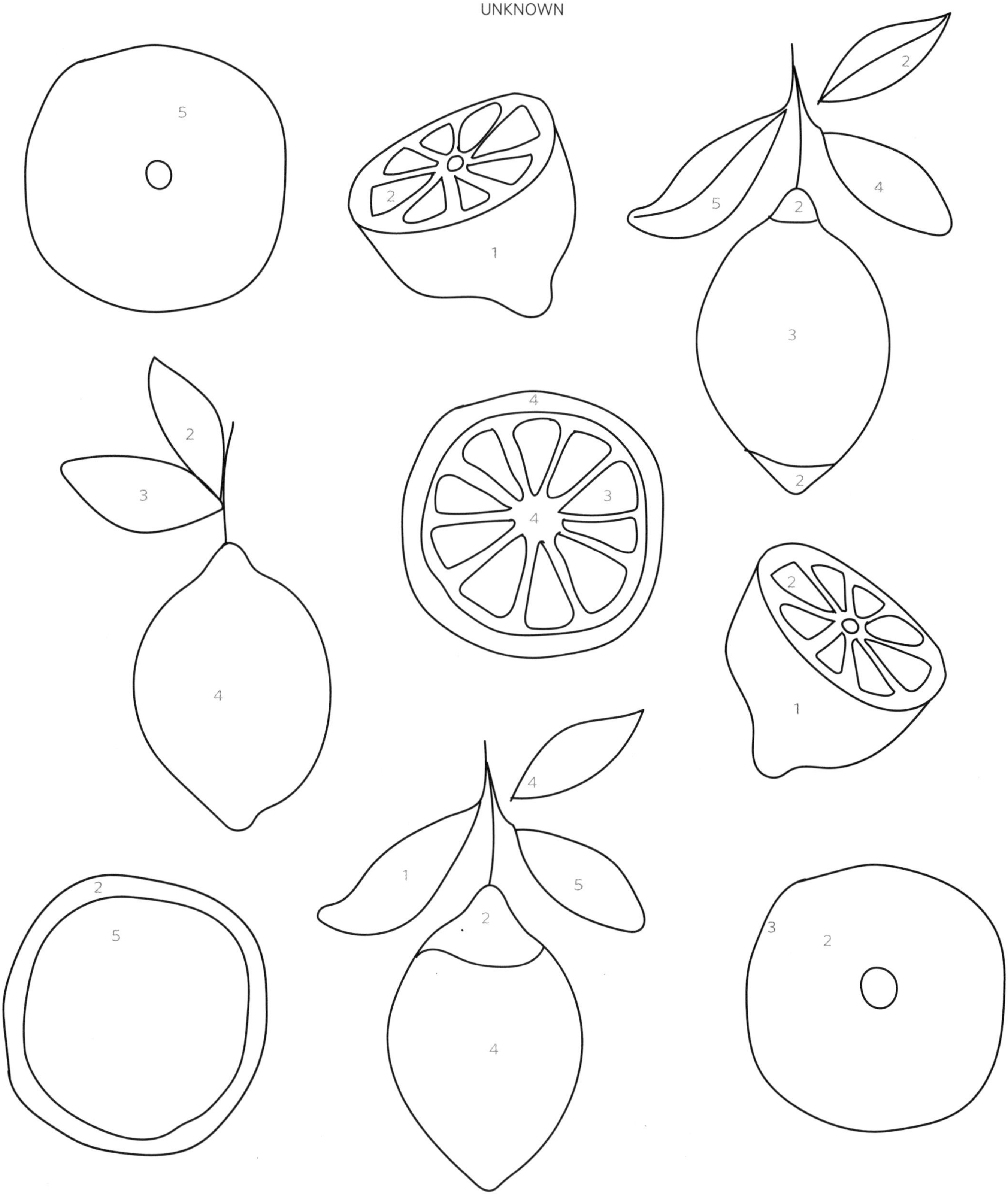

Follow the numbers to match your Doodles on the opposite page.

1 - Swirls   2 - Lines   3 - Circles   4 - Dashes   5 - Drops

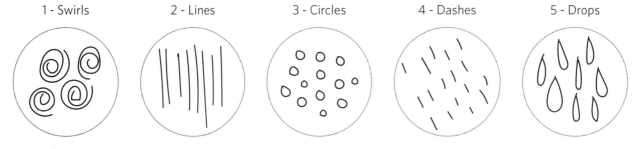

A bird doesn't sing because
it has an answer, it sings
because it has a song.

MAYA ANGELOU

Follow the numbers to match your Doodles on the opposite page.

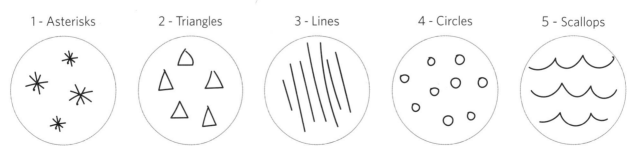

1 - Asterisks   2 - Triangles   3 - Lines   4 - Circles   5 - Scallops

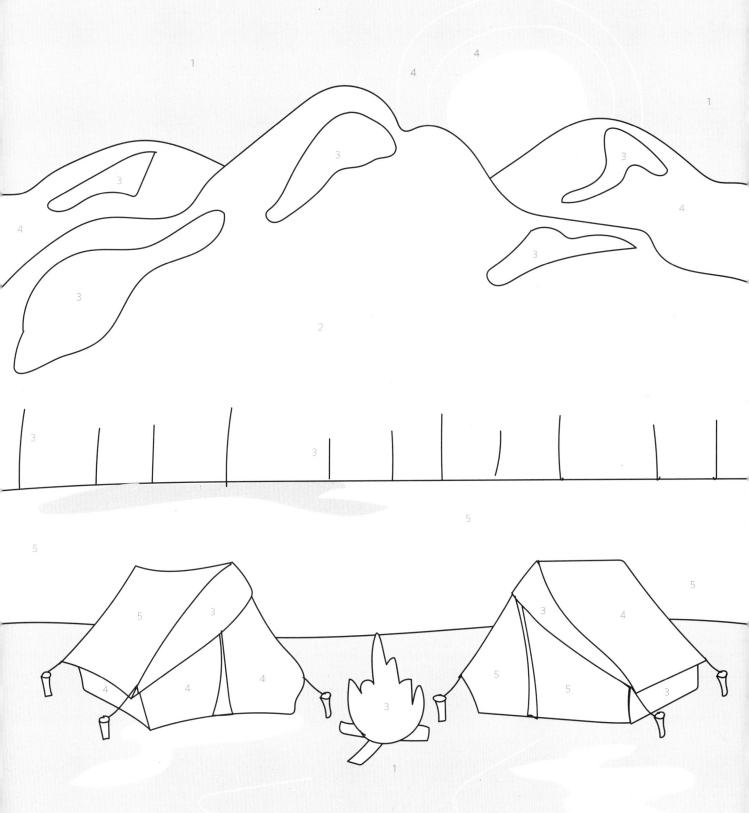

KEEP YOUR EYES ON THE STARS
AND YOUR FEET ON THE GROUND.

THEODORE ROOSEVELT

Follow the numbers to match your Doodles on the opposite page.

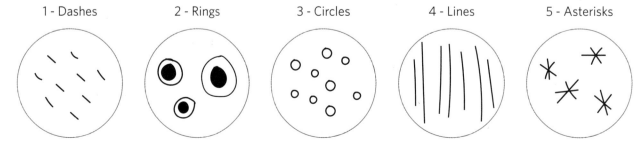

1 - Dashes   2 - Rings   3 - Circles   4 - Lines   5 - Asterisks

Art is a line around your thoughts.

GUSTAV KLIMT

Follow the numbers to match your Doodles on the opposite page.

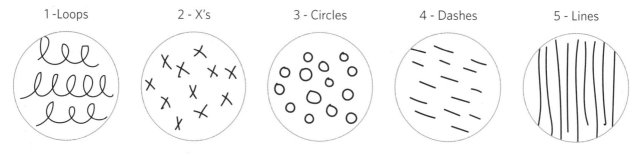

1 - Loops   2 - X's   3 - Circles   4 - Dashes   5 - Lines

THE WORLD ONLY EXISTS IN YOUR EYES.
YOU CAN MAKE IT AS BIG OR AS SMALL AS YOU WANT.

F. SCOTT FITZGERALD

Follow the numbers to match your Doodles on the opposite page.

1 - Squares   2 - Dashes   3 - V's   4 - Hearts   5 - Circles

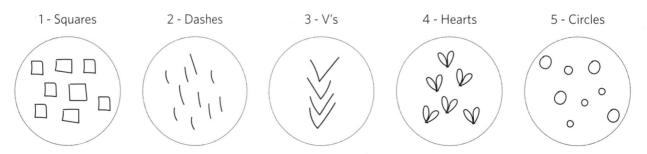

Wherever life plants you,
bloom with grace.

FRENCH PROVERB

Follow the numbers to match your Doodles on the opposite page.

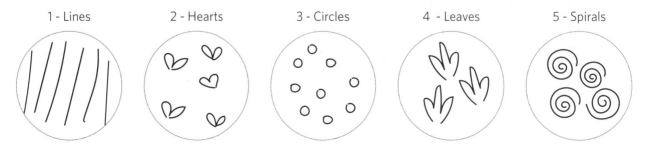

1 - Lines	2 - Hearts	3 - Circles	4 - Leaves	5 - Spirals

YOU ARE YOU. NOW, ISN'T THAT PLEASANT?

DR. SEUSS

Follow the numbers to match your Doodles on the opposite page.

1 - X's   2 - Circles   3 - Lines   4 - Scallops   5 - Asterisks

I believe, everyday, you should have one exquisite moment.

AUDREY HEPBURN

Meet the Doodler

MELISSA LLOYD is an international Doodler, designer,
teacher, author and inspirationalist. Her passion for
creativity can be found globally on products, environments
and in the hearts of those with whom she has connected.

Melissa combines her twenty plus years of experience
in professional design and communication with her passion
and connection to humanity, psychology, art therapy
and mindfulness; infusing a deep understanding of self.

Melissa teaches soul-care through creative practices and
encourages you to learn how to navigate the stormy seas of life,
reducing stress and rejuvenating your mind.

By honoring your creative soul and the celebration of
living in the moment, Melissa inspires you to bring joy back
into your life by finding a place of peace internally.
Her transformational approach to creativity, through Doodling
and living, inspires others to live a healthier and happier life.
'Always Be You… For You.'

Melissa splits her time between mothering, creating,
teaching and living in her little Cottage By The Sea.
To discover more of Melissa's work visit: doodlelovely.com

*Life is short,
make it sweet!*

Did you enjoy this *Doodle By Number*™? We would love to hear your feedback!
Please email us: **hello@doodlelovely.com**

Look for our next issue that will be filled with NEW Doodles.
This will be available in our Web Shop and in select stores across Canada.
www.doodlelovely.com